the
twenty-third psalm

AN INTERPRETATION

CHARLES L. ALLEN

FLEMING H. REVELL COMPANY
OLD TAPPAN, NEW JERSEY

Introduction

UNQUESTIONABLY the Twenty-third Psalm is one of the world's greatest gems. It would be impossible to imagine a collection of devotional classics or treasured Scriptures which omitted it. The child learns the Twenty-third Psalm at his mother's knee, and its strength reassures the bereaved who gather to remember a loved one. One of the masterpieces of Judaism, it seems to Christians so perfectly to portray their Master that some are surprised to learn it is not in the New Testament.

In this book Charles L. Allen points out the practical values of the Shepherd Psalm for the modern reader. One by one he lifts up its memorable phrases and shows how they can guide us through the valleys and bypaths of life into abiding peace and fulness of joy. Martin Luther used to say that the "hinge" of this Psalm is the word "my." Dr. Allen shows us how that personal pronoun throbs with life . . . "The power of the universe is power at *my* disposal."

Originally printed in *God's Psychiatry*, this interpretation of the Twenty-third Psalm has won acclaim from increasing multitudes of readers. We send it forth in this gift edition with the hope that it may cheer and inspire multitudes more.

THE PUBLISHERS

the twenty-third psalm

The Lord is my shepherd; I shall
not want.

He maketh me to lie down in green
pastures: he leadeth me beside the still
waters.

He restoreth my soul: he leadeth me
in the paths of righteousness for his
name's sake.

Yea, though I walk through the valley
of the shadow of death, I will fear no
evil: for thou art with me; thy rod and thy
staff they comfort me.

Thou preparest a table before me in
the presence of mine enemies: thou
anointest my head with oil; my cup runneth
over.

Surely goodness and mercy shall follow
me all the days of my life: and I will
dwell in the house of the Lord for ever.

a pattern of thinking

A MAN I admire very much came in to see me. Many years ago he started with his company at the bottom but with determination to get to the top. He has unusual abilities and energy and he used all he had. Today he is president of his company and he has all the things that go with his position.

Yet, along the way, he left out something, and one of the things he did not achieve is happiness. He was a nervous, tense, worried, and sick man. Finally, one of his physicians suggested that he talk with a minister.

We talked of how his physicians had given him prescriptions and he had taken them. Then I took a sheet of paper and wrote out my prescription for him. I prescribed the Twenty-third Psalm, five times a day for seven days.

I insisted that he take it just as I prescribed. He was to read it the first thing when he awakened in the morning—carefully, meditatively, and prayerfully. Immediately after breakfast, he was to do exactly the same thing. Also immediately after lunch, again after dinner, and, finally, just before he went to bed.

It was not to be a quick, hurried reading. He was to think about each phrase, giving his mind time to soak up as much of the meaning as possible. At the end of just one week, I promised, things would be different for him.

That prescription sounds simple, but really it isn't. The Twenty-third Psalm is one of the most powerful pieces of writing in existence, and it can do marvelous things for any person. I have suggested this to many people and in every instance in which I know it has been tried, it has produced results. It can change your life in seven days.

One man told me that he did not have time to read it during the day, so he just read it five times in the morning. However, when a physician prescribes a medicine after each meal, or every certain number of hours, no one would take the full day's dose at one time.

Some have told me that after two or three days they felt they knew it sufficiently, and thus, instead of taking time to read it thoughtfully, they would just think about it through the day. That won't work. To be most effective, it must be taken exactly as prescribed.

Ralph Waldo Emerson said, "A man is what he thinks about all day long." Marcus Aurelius said, "A man's life is what his thoughts make it." Norman Vincent Peale says, "Change your thoughts and you change your world." The Bible says, "For as he thinketh in his heart, so is he" (Proverbs 23:7).

The Twenty-third Psalm is a pattern of thinking, and when a mind becomes saturated with it, a new way of thinking and a new life are the result. It contains only 118 words. One could memorize it in a short time. In fact, most of us already know it. But its power is not in memorizing the words, but rather in thinking the thoughts.

The power of this Psalm lies in the fact that it represents a positive, hopeful, faith-approach to life. We assume it was written by David, the same David who had a black chapter of sin and failure in his life. But he spends no time in useless regret and morbid looking back.

David possesses the same spirit that St. Paul expresses: "Forgetting those things which are behind, and reaching forth unto those things which are before, I press toward the mark" (Philippians 3:13,14), or the spirit of our Lord when He said, "Neither do I condemn thee: go, and sin no more" (John 8:11).

Take it as I prescribe, and in seven days there will be deeply and firmly implanted within your mind a powerful new way of thinking that will bring marvelous changes in your outlook and give you a new life.

the lord
is my shepherd,
i shall not want

IMMEDIATELY after World War II the Allied armies gathered up many hungry, homeless children and placed them in large camps. There the children were abundantly fed and cared for. However, at night they did not sleep well. They seemed restless and afraid.

Finally, a psychologist hit on a solution. After the children were put to bed, they each received a slice of bread to hold. If they wanted more to eat, more was provided, but this particular slice was not to be eaten—it was just to hold.

The slice of bread produced marvelous results. The child would go to sleep, subconsciously feeling it would have something to eat tomorrow. That assurance gave the child a calm and peaceful rest.

15

In the Twenty-third Psalm, David points out something of the same feeling in the sheep when he says, "The Lord is my shepherd; I shall not want." Instinctively, the sheep knows the shepherd has made plans for its grazing tomorrow. He knows the shepherd made ample provision for it today, so will he tomorrow, so the sheep lies down in its fold with, figuratively speaking, the piece of bread in its hand.

So this Psalm does not begin with a petition asking God for something; rather it is a calm statement of fact—"The Lord *is* my shepherd." We do not have to beg God for things.

As Roy L. Smith and others have pointed out, God made provision for our needs long before we even had a need. Before we ever felt cold, God began storing up oil, coal, and gas to keep us warm. He knew we would be hungry, so, even before He put man on the earth, God put fertility into the soil and life into the seeds. "Your Father knoweth what things ye have need of, before ye ask him," said Jesus (Matthew 6:8).

The greatest source of human worry is about tomorrow, as it was with the women going to the tomb of Jesus on Easter morning. They missed the beauty of the early morning sun and the glory of the flowers along the way. They were worrying about who would roll away the stone. And when they got there it was already rolled away.

In another place (Psalm 37:25) David says, "I have been young, and now am old; yet have I not seen the righteous forsaken, nor his seed begging bread." Come to think about it, neither have I. Have you?

All life came from God. That includes my life. God keeps faith with fowls of the air and the grass of the field. And Jesus asks us to think that if God will do so much for a simple bird or a wild flower, how much more will He do for us (Matthew 6:25,34).

St. Paul says, "My God shall supply all your need" (Philippians 4:19). David puts it, "The Lord is my shepherd; I shall not want." With that faith we can work today without worrying about tomorrow.

he maketh me to lie down in green pastures

ONE morning as I was hurriedly dressing to begin a full and thrilling day, I felt a pain in my back. I mentioned it to my wife but was sure it would soon pass away. However, she insisted I see a physician, and he put me in a hospital.

In the hospital I was very unhappy. I had no time to waste there in bed. My calendar was full of good activities and the doctor had told me to cancel all my appointments for at least a month. A dear minister friend of mine came

to see me. He sat down and very firmly said, "Charles, I have only one thing to say to you— 'He *maketh* me to lie down.' "

I lay there thinking about those words in the Twenty-third Psalm long after my friend had gone. I thought about how the shepherd starts the sheep grazing about 4 o'clock in the morning. The sheep walk steadily as they graze; they are never still.

By 10 o'clock, the sun is beaming down and the sheep are hot, tired, and thirsty. The wise shepherd knows that the sheep must not drink when it is hot, neither when its stomach is filled with undigested grass.

So the shepherd makes the sheep lie down in green pastures, in a cool, soft spot. The sheep will not eat lying down, so he chews his cud, which is nature's way of digestion.

Study the lives of great people, and you will find every one of them drew apart from the hurry of life for rest and reflection. Great poems are not written on crowded streets, lovely songs are not written in the midst of clamoring multitudes; our visions of God come when we stop. The psalmist said, "Be still, and know that I am God" (Psalm 46:10).

Elijah found God, not in the earthquake or the fire, but in "a still small voice." Moses saw the burning bush as he was out on the hillside. Saul of Tarsus was on the lonely, quiet road to Damascus when he saw the heavenly vision. Jesus took time to be alone and to pray.

This is perhaps the most difficult thing for us to do. We will work for the Lord, we will sing, preach, teach. We will even suffer and sacrifice. Lustily we sing, "Work, for the night is coming," "Onward, Christian soldiers," "Stand up, stand up for Jesus."

We sometimes forget that before Jesus sent out His disciples to conquer the world, He told them to tarry for prayer and the power of God.

Sometimes God puts us on our backs in order to give us a chance to look up: "He maketh me to lie down." Many times we are forced, not by God, but by circumstances of one sort or another to lie down. That can always be a blessed experience. Even the bed of an invalid may be a blessing if he takes advantage of it!

Take from our souls the strain and stress,
And let our ordered lives confess
The beauty of thy peace. —WHITTIER

he leadeth me beside the still waters

THE sheep is a very timid creature. Especially is it afraid of swiftly moving water, which it has good reason to fear.

The sheep is a very poor swimmer because of its heavy coat of wool. The water soaks into

the sheep's coat and pulls it down. It is comparable to a man trying to swim with his overcoat on.

Instinctively, the sheep knows it cannot swim in swift current. The sheep will not drink from a moving stream. The sheep will drink only from still waters.

The shepherd does not laugh at the sheep's fears. He does not try to force the sheep. Instead, as he leads it across the mountains and valleys, he is constantly on the watch for still waters where its thirst may be quenched.

If there are no still waters available, while the sheep are resting, the shepherd will gather up stones to fashion a dam across a small stream to form a pool from which even the tiniest lamb may drink without fear.

This petition of the Twenty-third Psalm has wonderful meaning for us. God knows our limitations, and He does not condemn us because we have weaknesses. He does not force us where we cannot safely and happily go. God never demands of us work which is beyond our strength and abilities.

Instead, God is constantly ministering to our needs. He understands the loads upon our shoulders. He also knows where the places of nourishment and refreshment are located. It gives one confidence to know that even while he is sleeping, the Shepherd is working to prepare for his needs tomorrow.

We are told, "He will not suffer thy foot to be moved: he that keepeth thee will not slumber. Behold, he that keepeth Israel shall neither slumber nor sleep" (Psalm 121:3,4).

One of the finest ways to relieve a tension in your life is to picture still water clearly in your mind. Maybe a little lake nestling among some pines. Maybe a tiny, cool spring on some hillside. Maybe a calm sea with gentle, rippling waves.

After the picture becomes clear, start repeating and believing, "He leadeth me beside the still waters." Such an experience produces a marvelous surrender and trust that enables one to face the heat of the day confidently, knowing there is refreshing and relaxed power awaiting under the leadership of One wiser than we.

The great Martin Luther used to sing:

A mighty fortress is our God,
A bulwark never failing;
Our helper he, amid the flood
Of mortal ills prevailing.

That is the feeling David had when he wrote the Twenty-third Psalm.

As this Psalm saturates your mind it gives you that same assurance, too.

he RESTOReth my soul

A LETTER to me concludes with: "Life ended for me somewhere during these years . . . through a slow process. It took

years to stifle my faith; but now it is entirely
gone. . . . I am only a shell. Perhaps the
shell . . . [is] gone."

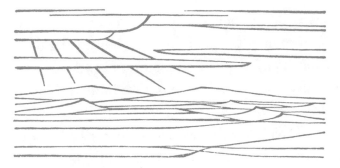

I would like to talk with the writer of that
letter about the meaning of David's words in
the Twenty-third Psalm, "He restoreth my
soul." David remembered that as the sheep start
out in the morning to graze, each takes a defi-
nite place in line and holds that same position
all during the day.

However, some time during the day each
sheep leaves its place in line and trots over to
the shepherd. The shepherd gently rubs its

nose and ears and whispers to it. Reassured and encouraged, the sheep takes its place in line again.

David remembered how close he once was to God, how God protected him as he went out to meet the giant Goliath, how God guided him along the way to success. Then David got busy. He was able to look after himself. He felt no need of God.

David lost his nearness to God. He did wrong. He became unhappy. His burden of guilt became too heavy to bear. Then he repented. God heard, forgave, and restored. He became a new man.

The human mind is like the human body. It can be wounded. Sorrow is a wound. It cuts deeply, but sorrow is a clean wound, and will heal unless something gets into the wound, such as bitterness, self-pity, or resentment.

Wrong is also a wound.

When I violate my standards I wound my

mind, and it is an unclean wound. Time will not heal that wound. Gradually, a sense of guilt can destroy a life and make it "only a shell." There is only one physician who can heal. The Fifty-first Psalm is the prayer David prayed.

"He restoreth my soul" can have another meaning. Moffatt translates it to read, "He revives life in me." Like a watch, the human spirit can just run down. We lose our drive and push. We become less willing to attempt the difficult. We are crusaders no longer.

Like squeezing the juice from an orange and leaving just the pulp, life has a way of squeezing the spirit out of a person. A person can become "only a shell." We feel the thrill of no new enthusiasm, the dawn of a new day leaves us cold and hopeless.

The Bible tells that God made the first man "and breathed into his nostrils the breath of life; and man became a living soul" (Genesis 2:7). And God has the power and the willingness to breathe a new breath of life into one who has lost.

Only God has the power. Speaking to a large number of physicians in Atlanta, Dr. R. B. Robins declared, "The psychiatrist's couch cannot take the place of the church in solving the problems of a frustrated society."

"He restoreth my soul"—"He revives life in me."

he leadeth me in the paths of righteousness for his name's sake

ON A plaque at Florida's Singing Tower you can read these words: "I come here to find myself. It is so easy to get lost in the world." That is true.

We come to the forks of life's road and cannot decide which way to turn. There are decisions to be made and yet it is so hard to decide

30

We do get lost. We need guidance, and David, in the Twenty-third Psalm, declares confidently, "He leadeth me in the paths of righteousness" (in the right paths).

Doubtless David remembers his own experiences as a shepherd. He knew that the sheep has no sense of direction. A dog, a cat, or a horse, if lost, can find its way back. They seem to have a compass within themselves. Not so with a sheep.

The sheep has very poor eyes. It cannot see ten or fifteen yards ahead. Palestinian fields were covered with narrow paths over which the shepherds led their sheep to pasture. Some of these paths led to a precipice over which the stupid sheep might fall to its death.

Other paths lead up a blind alley. But some paths lead to green pastures and still waters. The sheep followed the shepherd, knowing it was walking in the right path. Sometimes the shepherd led over steep and difficult places, but the paths he followed always ended up some-where.

The sheep was willing to trust that "some-where" to the shepherd's judgment. Even as we sing,

> Lord, I would clasp thy hand in
>   mine,
> Nor ever murmur nor repine;
> Content, whatever lot I see,
> Since 'tis my God that leadeth me.

Perhaps David remembered his forefathers as they made their way across a trackless wil-derness from Egypt to the Promised Land. God sent a pillar of fire by night and a pillar of cloud by day. Following it, the Israelites did come to the land they longed for.

For some the paths of righteousness mean hard going at times. Dr. Ralph W. Sockman tells about an English lad who decided to join the army for service in India. When asked the reason for his choice, he said: "I hear that in the

Indian army they pay you a lot for doing a little. When you get on further, they pay you more for doing less. When you retire, they pay you quite a lot for doing nothing."

Though God does not put a bed of roses on the battlefield or a carpet on the race track; though He does not promise us an easy, effortless life, He does promise us strength and He does promise to go with us.

Notice that the Psalm says, "He *leadeth* me." God doesn't drive. He is climbing the same hill that we climb—man is not alone. As we take life one step at a time, we can walk with Him the right paths.

The wise man says, "In all thy ways acknowledge him, and he shall direct thy paths" (Proverbs 3:6). That is true. The person who sincerely seeks to do God's will, whatever His will may be, will know the leadership of Eternal Wisdom.

He will lead you to your Promised Land.

yea, though i walk
through the valley of
the shadow of death,
i will fear no evil: for
thou art with me

LET me draw an illustration from the story
of a mother who collapsed when news
came that her son had been killed. She went
into her room, closed the door, and would see
no one.

Her minister came and sat down by her bed-
side, but she would not speak to him. For a little
while all was quiet and then slowly he began
saying, "The Lord is my shepherd; I shall not
want." Phrase by phrase, he gently spoke the
words of the Psalm, and she listened.

When he came to that great phrase of comfort, she joined in and together they said, "Yea,
though I walk through the valley of the shadow of

35

death, I will fear no evil: for thou art with me."

A smile flickered on her lips, and she said, "I see it differently now."

Henry Ward Beecher says the Twenty-third Psalm is the nightingale of the Psalms. The nightingale sings its sweetest when the night is darkest. And for most of us death is the most terrifying fact of life.

After a funeral, someone said to me, "You conduct a lot of funerals; doesn't it become routine for you?" The answer is no. You never become accustomed to death. Each one is a new and fresh experience.

We bring our flowers and we have lovely music, but not even flowers and music can make a tomb a place of cheer. And death makes us afraid. We feel so helpless and alone.

Of course, "the valley of the shadow of death" refers to more than the actual experiences of physical death. It has been translated, "the glen of gloom." It might be applicable to every hard and terrifying experience of life.

The Basque Sheepherder describes an actual Valley of the Shadow of Death in Palestine. It leads from Jerusalem to the Dead Sea and is a very narrow and dangerous pathway through the mountain range. The path is rough, and there is danger that a sheep may fall to its death at any moment.

It is a forbidding journey that one dreads to take. But the sheep is not afraid. Why? Because the shepherd is with it.

And so come those dark places in life through which we are compelled to pass. Death is one. Disappointment is another. Loneliness is another. There are many more.

I have told many people in "the valley of the shadow" to get off by themselves in a quiet place. Quit struggling for a little while. Forget the many details. Stop your mind for a little while from hurrying on to the morrow and to next year and beyond.

Just stop, become still and quiet, and in the midst of your "glen of gloom" you will feel a strange and marvelous presence more powerfully than you have ever felt it before. Many have told me of feeling that presence—of hearing the nightingale sing in the darkness.

Wherever my pathway leads, I will not be afraid, said David, and countless multitudes also have rid themselves of fear. Why? "For thou art with me." There is power in His presence.

thy rod and thy staff they comfort me

I ONCE knew a man who was hurt badly in a cyclone. From then on much of the joy of life was gone for him, not because of his injury, but rather because he was afraid that another cyclone might come. There was nothing he could do.

He worried because there was still nothing he would be able to do if he saw another cyclone coming—until one day his children decided to build a cyclone cellar. They completed it and the man looked at it with relaxed joy. Now, no matter how hard a cyclone blew, he had protection. It was a great comfort to him.

In the Twenty-third Psalm we read, "Thy rod and thy staff they comfort me." The sheep is a helpless animal. It has no weapon with which to fight. It is easy prey to any wild beast of the field. It is afraid.

But the shepherd carries a rod, which is a heavy, hard club two to three feet long. When David wrote this Psalm he probably remembered his own need for such a rod. In I Samuel 17, David tells Saul how he slew a lion and a bear in protecting his sheep.

Also, the shepherd carried a staff, which was about eight feet long. The end of the staff was turned into a crook. Many paths in Palestine were along the steep sides of mountains. The sheep would lose its footing and slip down, hanging helplessly on some ledge below.

With his staff the shepherd could reach down, place the crook over the small chest of the sheep and lift it back onto the pathway. The sheep instinctively is comforted by the shepherd's rod and staff. It is the comfort of knowing that the shepherd will be able to meet an emergency.

I have insurance on my automobile. I hope I will never need it, but I am comforted by the fact that I do have it.

I regret that my country finds it necessary to spend so much money on military preparedness. Yet, when I think of the condition of the world, my country's strength comforts me.

There are needs of my life that I cannot meet, and, like St. Paul it comforts me to say, "Now unto him that is able to do exceeding abundantly above all that we ask or think" (Ephesians 3:20).

Seemingly there is overwhelming evil in the world. We are a scared people. Many times we feel helpless; then we find comfort in realizing the power of God.

Certainly I do not think of God as just a cyclone cellar or an insurance policy. Yet I can say with James Montgomery:

> *God is my strong salvation;*
> *what foe have I to fear?*
> *In darkness and temptation,*
> *my light, my help is near.*
> *Though hosts encamp around me,*
> *firm in the fight I stand;*
> *What terror can confound me,*
> *with God at my right hand?*

"Thy rod and thy staff"—that takes a lot of the dread and fear of the future out of my heart.

thou preparest a table before me in the presence of mine enemies

IN ONE town where we lived there arose an issue over whether or not a poolroom should be permitted to open. My father vigorously

crusaded against it, and I remember someone rather jokingly asked him if he thought he would be tempted to play pool.

He said no, but that he had some boys and he did not want his boys in a poolroom. He might have kept his boys away, but he felt it would be safer to keep the poolroom away. My father's feeling in the matter serves to illustrate what David meant in the Twenty-third Psalm when he said: "Thou preparest a table before me in the presence of mine enemies."

In the pastures of the Holy Land grew poisonous plants which were fatal to the sheep if eaten. Also, there were plants whose sharp thorns would penetrate the soft noses of the sheep and cause ugly sores.

Each spring the shepherd would take his mattock and dig out these enemies of the sheep, pile them up and burn them. Thus the pastures were safe for the sheep to graze. The pasture became, as it were, a table prepared. The present enemies were destroyed by the shepherds.

We constantly must do this for our children. When my children go and come from school, a policewoman stands on the corner. She is there to protect my children.

Happily, in our city our school children have not yet been faced with a serious dope situation. But I want my city to keep it that way, exercising all possible vigilance. I feel the same way about obscene literature and many other things that harm and destroy life. We must constantly crusade against the enemies of life.

It is not enough for the farmer to plant his seed. He must go through his crop again and again to destroy the weeds. So must the spirit of God in man militantly crusade. It is not enough just to preach the gospel. We must destroy the enemies.

Recently my children were vaccinated against some disease. I thank medical science for going before to prevent or destroy the cause of the disease. Parents, scientists, government, society as a whole, must prepare a table, destroying the enemies, so that all good life may be safely nourished.

After a sermon on race prejudice, a good man took me to task for not preaching the gospel. But I have seen prejudice and false ideas of racial superiority destroy the opportunities for children of God. I feel my sermon was a compulsory part of the gospel.

It is not enough just to sit around piously being good. There are times when "the Son of God goes forth to war."

One other thought—Jesus expresses the petition of David when He prays, "Lead us not into temptation." As we move along through life, we know there will be enemies seeking to destroy. Many worry because of a fear they will not be able to hold out—the fear of failure and of falling.

But the Shepherd of men is out ahead, and

we can be assured of the protection of His strength. There is "the victory that overcometh the world, even our faith" (I John 5:4).

thou anointest my head with oil; my cup runneth over

I WILL never forget what the coach said to us the first day I went out for football practice. He told us that football is a rough game and that if we expected to play it, we must also expect sometimes to get hurt.

So with life. If you expect to live it, you must also expect some bruises and hurt. That is just the way it is. And David, thinking of that fact, said in the Twenty-third Psalm, "Thou anointest my head with oil; my cup runneth over."

Sometimes, as the sheep grazed, its head would be cut by the sharp edge of a stone buried in the grass. There were other potential dangers—briars to scratch and thorns to stick.

Then, some days the sheep had to walk steep paths under a hot, merciless sun. At the end of the day it would be tired and spent.

So the shepherd would stand at the door of the fold and examine each sheep as it came in. If there were hurt places the shepherd would apply soothing and healing oil. Instead of becoming infected, the hurt would soon heal.

Also, the shepherd had a large earthen jug of water, the kind of a jar which kept the water refreshingly cool through evaporation. As the sheep came in, the shepherd would dip down into the water with his big cup and bring it up brimful. The tired sheep drank deeply of the life-quickening draught.

Remember how, as little children, we would bruise a finger or stub a toe? We would come running to Mama, who would kiss the hurt away. There was mystic healing in her loving concern.

As older children we still get hurt. A heart can be broken, a conscience can ache like an infected tooth, feelings can be hurt, the world can deal cruelly and harshly. One can become discouraged and tired. Sometimes the burden of life can be unbearable.

But also there is the tender Shepherd who understands the hurt of His children and is ever ready and able to minister to that hurt. Harry Lauder, the famous Scotch comedian, was grief-stricken at the loss of his son. But he found the Shepherd. Later, he was giving a concert in Chicago before an overflow crowd. He responded to repeated encores, and finally he quieted the audience and said very quietly, "Don't thank me. Thank the good God who put the songs in my heart."

Notice David said, "Thou anointest *my* head with oil; *my* cup. . . ." He didn't say "our" heads. It is the singular pronoun. All day long the shepherd has been concerned with the flock. But as they go into the fold he takes them one by one.

I had a professor in college one year who never did learn my name. Somehow, I never liked him very much. I read that Jesus said, "He calleth his own sheep by name" (John 10:3). I like that. It makes me feel important.

The psalmist said, "He healeth the broken in heart. . . . He telleth the number of the stars" (Psalm 147:3,4). The power of the universe is power at *my* disposal.

surely goodness and mercy shall follow me all the days of my life

IN THE play "South Pacific," Mary Martin sang a song that I think is wonderful. In that song she sang: "I'm stuck like a dope, with a thing called hope, I can't get it out of my heart."

David says the same thing in different words: "Surely goodness and mercy shall follow me all the days of my life." He is not wistfully thinking. He says *surely . . . surely . . . surely.*

David was an old man when he wrote the Twenty-third Psalm. He had seen tragedies and disappointments, but he also had come to know God—a God who knows the needs of His children and who abundantly provides for those needs, a God who can restore life and take away fear. In spite of dark clouds on the horizon, with a God like Him whom David knew, David was sure the sun would shine tomorrow.

We hear a lot about the wickedness of men and the destruction of the world. We know of bombs which can destroy cities with one awful blast. We tremble at the sound of dire predictions of the vengeful judgment of God. But, somehow, as our minds are filled with the picture of the loving Shepherd leading His sheep, we feel confident that He will lead us through the dark valleys.

One of the greatest teachers America has ever produced was Professor Endicott Peabody, headmaster of Groton for many years. One day at chapel he told his boys, "Remember, things in life will not always run smoothly. . . . The great fact to remember is that the trend of civilization is forever upward."

Those words stuck in the mind of one of his students, and about forty years later that student gave new heart to the nation when he said, "The only thing to fear is fear itself." Franklin D. Roosevelt will always be remembered for the hope he gave to a hopeless nation.

Many people think themselves into disaster. They feel a little bad and they fill their minds with the thought of being sick. They start out the day with dread of something bad happening. They look to tomorrow with fear and trembling.

There is a very successful teacher I have read about who teaches people to sit quietly and conceive of their minds as being absolutely blank. Then he tells them to think of the mind as being a motion-picture screen, and to flash on that screen a picture of something good they want to happen. Then he suggests that they flash the picture on and off, repeating that process until the picture becomes clear and sharp, and firmly established in the conscious and subconscious mind. Then the professor tells the students to go to work to make that picture a reality, to maintain a spirit of prayer and faith.

It is amazing how completely and how quickly that picture in the mind will be developed in life.

Quit predicting disaster for your world and yourself. Say with the psalmist,

(Psalm 118:24).

Begin the morning with hope. Plant this

firmly in your mind, "Surely goodness and mercy shall follow me," and they will.

and i will dwell in the house of the lord for ever

IT IS always a thrilling experience to me to be downtown about 5 o'clock in the afternoon. The streets are filled with people and cars. Extra buses are running, and every one is packed with people standing.

It is thrilling because the people are going home.

John Howard Payne had been away from home for nine years. One afternoon he stood at the window watching the throngs of people, happy, hurrying, going home. Suddenly he felt lonely, there in a Paris boardinghouse room.

Impatiently he turned from the window. He had work to do. It was perhaps an important

play he was writing. He had no time for sentimental dreaming. But the mood and the memories of a little town on Long Island would not leave him.

He picked up a pencil and began writing:

Mid pleasures and palaces though
we may roam,
Be it ever so humble, there's no
place like home.

And now for more than a hundred years that song has had a special place in the hearts of the people. There really is "no place like home."

But I also feel sadness as I watch the crowds going home. I know some who have no home to which to go. Some wander around seeking a cheap bed for the night, others can afford the nicest hotel suite in the city—still it isn't home.

I have dealt with a lot of alcoholics. Especially have a number of women told me how they started. They would go to an empty cheerless room or small apartment, and be alone.

There is not much fun in living alone. So many started drinking that way.

Much, much more pathetic than seeing a homeless person at the end of the day is to find a person who is not sure of God and has no hope of the eternal home, who at the close of life's day can look forward only to some dark grave and oblivion.

David closes the Twenty-third Psalm with a mighty crescendo of faith when he declares, "I will dwell in the house of the Lord for ever."

One of the heart-stirring passages in Bunyan's *Pilgrim's Progress* is that in which "Mr. Feeble Mind" speaks of his hope of home. He says:

But this I have resolved on, to wit, to run when I can, to go when I cannot run, and to creep when I cannot go. . . . My mind is beyond the river that has no bridge, though I am, as you see, but of a feeble mind.

Sometimes the greatest inspiration for living

comes when your "mind is beyond the river that has no bridge." Were it not for that assurance, many experiences of life would be unbearable.

David did not have the insights that we have. He never heard the words: "I am the resurrection, and the life: he that believeth in me, though he were dead, yet shall he live: and whosoever liveth and believeth in me shall never die" (John 11:25,26).

Just knowing intimately a God such as he describes in the Twenty-third Psalm gave David assurance that at the close of life's day he would go home.

"he knows the shepherd"

THERE is a story—I do not know its source —of an old man and a young man on the same platform before a vast audience of people.

A special program was being presented. As a part of the program each was to repeat from memory the words of the Twenty-third Psalm. The young man, trained in the best speech technique and drama, gave in the language of the ancient silver-tongued orator the words of the Psalm.

"The Lord is my shepherd. . . ." When he had finished, the audience clapped their hands and cheered, asking him for an encore so that they might hear again his wonderful voice.

Then the old gentleman, leaning heavily on his cane, stepped to the front of the same platform, and in feeble, shaking voice repeated the same words—"The Lord is my shepherd. . . ."

But when he was seated no sound came from the listeners. Folks seemed to pray. In the silence the young man stood to make the following statement:

"Friends," he said, "I wish to make an explanation. You asked me to come back and repeat the Psalm, but you remained silent when my friend here was seated. The difference? I shall tell you. I know the Psalm, but he knows the Shepherd!"

Perhaps the figure of the shepherd and the flock may mean little to the modern city dweller. Yet, if ever a people of this earth resembled a flock of frightened sheep it is now. Governments are afraid of each other. People are afraid of their governments, of other people, and of themselves.

This Psalm of David has sung its way across the barriers of time, race, and language. For twenty-five centuries it has been treasured in the hearts of people. Today it is more beloved than ever before.

The reason it lives? Not just because it is great literature. Because it tells that above all the strife and fears, the hungers and weaknesses of mankind, there is a Shepherd—a Shepherd who knows His sheep one by one, who is abundantly able to provide, who guides and protects and at the close of the day opens the door to the sheepfold—the house not made with hands.

In the quietness of the South Pole Admiral Byrd suddenly realized he was "not alone." That assurance caused faith to well up within him, and even though he stood in "the coldest cold on the face of the earth," he felt a comforting warmth.

The Twenty-third Psalm gives men that same assurance. That is why it lives in the hearts of men, regardless of race or creed.